DATE DUE			MAR 0 4
GAYLORD			PRINTED IN U.S.A.

HOME

HOME

A COLLECTION OF POETRY & ART

EDITED BY
STAN TYMOREK

HARRY N. ABRAMS, INC., PUBLISHERS

For JAN

PROJECT MANAGER: Margaret Rennolds Chace
EDITOR: Elisa Urbanelli
DESIGNER: Darilyn Lowe Carnes

Library of Congress Cataloging-in-Publication Data

Home : a collection of poetry & art / edited by Stan Tymorek.
   p. cm.
  ISBN 0–8109–3435–3
  1. Home—Poetry.   I. Tymorek, Stan.
 PN6110.H6H66 1999
  700'.455—DC21   99–13453

Page 1: Jan Tymorek. *Barbara's Hydrangeas.* 1998

Page 2: George Loftus Noyes. *The Gorge* (detail). 1912.
Oil on canvas, 30½ x 34¼". Private Collection, California

Published in 1999 by Harry N. Abrams, Incorporated, New York

Printed and bound in Hong Kong

 Harry N. Abrams, Inc.
100 Fifth Avenue
New York, N.Y. 10011
www.abramsbooks.com

ACKNOWLEDGMENTS

As this is my first book, I would like to acknowledge those who have taught me the most: Stanley P. Tymorek, Rob Tarule, Richard Grossinger, Archie Lieberman, and Al Shackelford.

Model anthologies, in which I also found home poems, were *The Rattle Bag*, edited by Seamus Heaney and Ted Hughes; *Technicians of the Sacred*, edited by Jerome Rothenberg; and *America: A Prophecy*, edited by Rothenberg and George Quasha. *The Poetics of Space*, by Gaston Bachelard, was also an inspiration.

I would like to thank the many contributing poets and artists who encouraged me during this project. In addition, Mike Kelly was instrumental in getting it off the ground. Jonathan Greene supplied several leads. Cid Corman very generously gave permissions and suggested the work of fellow poets. And Catherine Bonnard Sullivan knew of just the right Magritte.

At Abrams, it was my pleasure to work with Margaret Rennolds Chace, who was an early believer; Elisa Urbanelli, my enthusiastic editor; and Darilyn Carnes, the book's designer. Thanks to all of you!

Above all, I want to thank Jan Ettlinger Tymorek, my wife, who contributed not only her photographs but her invaluable assistance with obtaining permissions. This book, which is in part hers, is dedicated entirely to her—with all my love.

S. T.

INTRODUCTION

The only time most of us wax poetic about our houses is when we are trying to sell them. Real-estate ads are an ongoing anthology of these effusions, filled with "breathtaking views," "charming woodwork," and that euphemism for all manner of down-at-the-mouth dwellings, "the handyman special."

So when you read in this collection of Robert Creeley describing his house as "this aged box," there is clearly another intention at play. The poet uses language to locate himself in the world and to praise the protection from the vicissitudes of the world outside:

> Hold on, dear house,
>
> 'gainst the long hours
> of emptiness, against
> the wind's tearing force.
>
> You are my mind
> made particular,
> my heart in its place.

The stereotypical poet's home is the garret, preferably unheated to increase the suffering for one's art. And you will find one here, sparely yet lovingly described by Patrick Kavanagh in "My Room." Yet you will also discover this collection makes up a quite diverse neighborhood of houses, including an igloo, a Hebridean house, a thirteenth-century Japanese hut, a boardinghouse, a spaceship, a castle in Spain, and several homes that sound like the types of places most of us live in. In some cases the poets have not actually inhabited the houses they write about, but have entered them with that always useful key, the imagination.

Another popular image of the poet, that of the wandering minstrel bent on steering clear of anything as mundane as a mortgage, is contradicted by several well-entrenched homebodies whose work is anthologized here. Take William Butler Yeats, author of the popular "The Song of Wandering Aengus." As Seamus Heaney tells it in *Writers and Their Houses*, Yeats was so caught up in the restoration of his home at Thoor Ballylee that he planned to inscribe in one of its stones a curse on heirs who would "alter for the worse" his beloved abode.

This project was first suggested by a number of "home poems" I had stumbled upon over the years; the accompanying images came later. Finding images to complement the poems became an exciting form of house-hunting, and I hope encountering the poems and images as neighbors helps readers feel more at home with the book.

Obviously, the houses of fiction—like *Bleak House, The House of Mirth,* and *The House of the Seven Gables*—are much better known than these houses of poetry. In collecting them under one roof, I was reminded of those odd but beautiful old farmhouses left standing alone and incongruous alongside of new housing developments, industrial parks, and interstate highways. Somehow, despite the threat of "progress," they survive. May these poems do the same.

S. T.

S. D. Butcher. *J. C. Cram Family, Sod House, Loup County, Nebraska.* 1886. S. D. Butcher Collection, Nebraska State Historical Society

"I Years had been from Home"
Emily Dickinson

I Years had been from Home
And now before the Door
I dared not enter, lest a Face
I never saw before

Stare stolid into mine
And ask my Business there—
"My Business but a Life I left
Was such remaining there?"

I leaned upon the Awe—
I lingered with Before—
The Second like an Ocean rolled
And broke against my ear—

I laughed a crumbling Laugh
That I could fear a Door
Who Consternation compassed
And never winced before.

I fitted to the Latch
My Hand, with trembling care
Lest back the awful Door should spring
And leave me in the Floor—

Then moved my Fingers off
As cautiously as Glass
And held my ears, and like a Thief
Fled gasping from the House—

William Christenberry. *Green Door, Newbern, Alabama.* 1997. Courtesy Pace Wildenstein MacGill Gallery

Interior of Emily Dickinson's House.
Courtesy of the Jones Library, Inc.,
Amherst, Massachusetts

EMILY DICKINSON'S HOUSE

(for Sam and Ann)
Michael McClure

WITHOUT PROPERTY CAN WE
BE REAL?
How can we feel
the unknown facets
of ourselves
without a parcel
of hard property?
Look there's a tanager
and also indigo buntings
in the sunset!
Waterfalls
cataract
upon the mind.
See,
the star
that touches us
with hands of light.

The house we live in
is delight.

THIS HOUSE

Robert Creeley

Such familiar space
out there, the window
frame's locating

focus I could
walk holding
on to

through air from
here to there,
see it where

now fog's close
denseness floats
the hedgerow up

off apparent ground,
the crouched, faint
trees lifting up

from it, and more
close down
there in front

by roof's slope, down,
the stonewall's conjoining,
lax boulders sit,

years' comfortable pace
unreturned, placed
by deliberation and

limit make their
sprawled edge. Here
again inside

the world one thought of,
placed in this aged box
moved here from

family site
lost as us, time's
spinning confusions

are what
one holds on to.
Hold on, dear house,

'gainst the long hours
of emptiness, against
the wind's tearing force.

You are my mind
made particular,
my heart in its place.

Charles Burchfield. *Noontide in Late May*. 1917.
Watercolor and gouache on paper, 22 x 17 7/8".
Whitney Museum of American Art, New York

Pudlo Pudlat. *Spirits*. 1966. Stonecut.
Reproduced with the permission of the
West Baffin Eskimo Co-operative, Ltd.

WHEN HOUSES WERE ALIVE

Told by Inugpasugjuk
Translated from the Inuktitut by
Knud Rasmussen and William Worster

One night a house suddenly rose up from the ground and went floating through the air. It was dark, & it is said that a swishing, rushing noise was heard as it flew through the air. The house had not yet reached the end of its road when the people inside begged it to stop. So the house stopped.

They had no blubber when they stopped. So they took soft, freshly drifted snow & put it in their lamps, & it burned.

They had come down at a village. A man came to their house & said:

Look, they are burning snow in their lamps. Snow can burn.

But the moment these words were uttered, the lamp went out.

"New-sawed"
Lorine Niedecker

New-sawed
clean-smelling house
sweet cedar pink
      flesh tint
I love you

Paul Rocheleau. *Attic of Wash House, built in 1854 by North Family Shakers, Mount Lebanon, New York.* 1994

THE HOUSE IN WINTER

Jane Hirshfield

Here,
in the year's late tidewash,
a corner cupboard suddenly wavers
in low-flung sunlight,
cupboard never quite visible before.

Its jars
of last summer's peaches
have come into their native gold—
not the sweetness of last summer,
but today's,
fresh from the tree of winter.
The mouth swallows *peach,* and says *gold.*

Though they dazzle and are gone,
the halves of fruit, the winter light,
the cupboard it has swept back into shadow.

As inhaled swiftly or slowly,
the sweet-wood scent goes out the same—
saying, *not world but the bright self breathing;*
saying, *not self but the world's bright breath.*
Saying finally, always, *gone,*
the deep shelves of systole and diastole empty.

Or perhaps it is
that the house only constructs itself
while we look—
opens, room from room, *because* we look.
The wood, the glass, the linens, flinging themselves
into form at the clap of our footsteps.
As the hard-dormant
peach tree wades into blossom and leaf
at the spring sun's knock: neither surprised
nor expectant, but every cell awakened at that knock.

Mary Azarian. *Pantry*. 1989.
Woodcut, 10 x 14"

21

Sheng Mou (Chinese,
active c. 1330–69).
*Enjoying Fresh Air in a
Mountain Retreat*. Yüan
Dynasty (1271–1368).
Hanging scroll, ink and
color on silk, 47½ x 22⅛".
The Nelson-Atkins
Museum of Art Kansas
City, Missouri. Purchase:
Nelson Trust

WHITE CRANE HILL

Su Tung-Po

Translated from the Chinese by Burton Watson

At my new place at White Crane Hill we dug a well
forty feet deep. We struck a layer of rock partway down,
but finally broke through and got to water.

Seacoast wears you out with damp and heat;
My new place is better—high and cool.
In return for the sweat of hiking up and down
I've a dry spot to sleep and sit.
But paths to the river are a rocky hell;
I wince at the water bearer's aching back.
I hired four men, put them to work
Hacking through layers of obdurate rock.
Ten days and they'd gone only eight or ten feet;
Below was a stratum of solid blue stone.
Drills all day struck futile sparks—
When would we ever see springs bubble up?
I'll keep you filled with rice and wine,
You keep your drills and hammers flying!
Mountain rock must end some time—
Stubborn as I am, I won't give up.
This morning the houseboy told me with joy
They're into dirt soft enough to knead!
At dawn the pitcher brought up milky water;
By evening, it was clearer than an icy stream.
All my life has been like this—
What way to turn and not run into blocks?
But Heaven has sent me a dipper of water;
Arm for a pillow, my happiness overflows.

Paul Rocheleau. *Double Crib House, West Side, The Homeplace—1850, Land Between the Lakes, Tennessee.* 1994

From THE ARK UPON HIS SHOULDERS

Forrest Gander

My husband did all this.   We used to live
in a rambling kind of house   with gossipy verandas.
Then he bought a stove, an iron stove   with a reservoir to it.
He always insisted it was bad luck   to come in that door
and go out the other. It's bad luck   to pay back salt
if you borrow it.   To the day he died
he smelled   pulled up from the dirt. He worked
the Norfolk Southern forty years   walking on top
of freight trains. I've seen him   up there
and the wind just blowing—   you could see the wind
blowing his clothes.
          Our second house   he built it.
Cut me a yard broom   from dogwood bushes,
tied in three places. Hogs   squealed under the floorboards
in winter—you could see one   through the cracks.
He had something he said   to hush them.
Come up the porch steps   arms full of lightwood.
In those days   we drank good old cool water
out of the well—cool and   put some syrup in it
and stir it up   and drink it right along
with our dinner. The summers were   so hot you saw
little devils   twizzling out in front of you.
He called them   lazy jacks. It was the heat.
Listen at that bird,   he'd say. It's telling us,
Love one another.

MY HOUSE NEW-PAINTED

William Bronk

The splendor is not surprising; we expected it
and shine in the brightness of new paint. That the lines
should firm, though, corners sharpen, and the eaves
be reasserted, is more than we thought to ask
or look for. What is shown is a strength of the house itself
that it held in its underframing, still could hold.

We hold houses in a kind of contempt and give
them nothing, or say we do, as a way to despise
the kinds of things that houses are, all
such kinds of things, the measured entities,
that they should not be what was intended: they fail.
They burn. They fade and sag. They fall away.
We think of a time before we housed the world
or gathered things—spirits were all we saw,
spirit was real, was what there was, was all.
This was man did this, and thought to do well
when he turned away to say, on the contrary, all
the world was what we measured: houses, sums
and angles, vectors and smoothable curves. We turn,
and turn again another way to find
some way to state the world, dissatisfied
none answers.

Still, I am pleased that my
particular house, not any way notable even,
has stood a hundred years and more, and firmed
by its shiny paint, should show the metaphor
of a material world, though it is plainly that
and nothing more—as spirit was nothing more—
could have such power now, summon it
as though from an actual world it meant to claim.
There is a world. This house can say there is.

William Christenberry. *Tenant House II*. 1960.
Oil on canvas, 79½ x 77¾". Morris Museum of
Art, Augusta, Georgia

Jan Tymorek. *Barbara's Hydrangeas.* 1998

PRIZE

Bob Arnold

Away from the road,
Off into the high edge
Of the field, unless I
Looked carefully you
Would never have been seen
Picking the wildflowers
Growing in folds of sunlight
Among the tall grass.

Each snipped by hand
At the same height, then
Gathered inside a pail
Of shallow water.

The world seems weightless
Watching you work,
If this is work—
You call it a prize
Saved for the last
Hour of the afternoon.
Taking away what this
Plot of land has to give—
Flowers for the kitchen table,
Brightened windowsills.

LANDLADY

P. R. Page

Through sepia air the boarders come and go
impersonal as trains. Pass silently
the craving silence swallowing her speech;
click doors like shutters on her camera eye.

Because of her their lives become exact:
their entrances and exits are designed;
phone calls are cryptic. Oh, her ticklish ears
advance and fall back stunned.

Nothing is unprepared. They hold the walls
about them when they weep or laugh. Each face
is dialled to zero publicly. She peers
stippled with curious flesh;

pads on the patient landing like a pulse,
unlocks their keyholes with the wire of sight,
searches their rooms for clues when they are out,
pricks when they come home late.

Wonders when they are quiet, jumps when they move,
dreams that they dope or drink, trembles to know
the traffic of their brains, jaywalks their street
in clumsy shoes.

Yet knows them better than their closest friends:
their cupboards and the secrets of their drawers,
their books, their private mail, their photographs
are theirs and hers.

Knows when they wash, how frequently their clothes
go to the cleaners, what they like to eat,
their curvature of health, but even so
is not content,

and, like a lover, must know all, all, all.
Prays she may catch them unprepared at last
and palm the dreadful riddle of their skulls—
hoping the worst.

John McCrady. *I Can't Sleep.*
1948. Multi-stage on canvas,
35½ x 47½". Morris Museum
of Art, Augusta, Georgia

HOW TO FIND US

Jonathan Greene

Down roads that snake
over ridges, going
nowhere fast.

Past orchestras of cars
spread on hillsides,
fading inventories.

Past abandoned houses
cows crowd in for shade.

Alongside ditches
beer cans call home.

Through gates
in stone walls
slaves built.

On to a road that has
spiked mufflers, broken
springs, given wheels
minds of their own.

Arrive in a wide expanse
of bottom surrounded
by hill & river
that took our breath away
at first seeing.

George Loftus Noyes. *The Gorge*. 1912. Oil on canvas,
30½ x 34¼". Private Collection, California

TOR HOUSE

Robinson Jeffers

If you should look for this place after a handful of lifetimes:
Perhaps of my planted forest a few
May stand yet, dark-leaved Australians or the coast cypress, haggard
With storm-drift; but fire and the axe are devils.
Look for foundations of sea-worn granite, my fingers had the art
To make stone love stone, you will find some remnant.
But if you should look in your idleness after ten thousand years:
It is the granite knoll on the granite
And lava tongue in the midst of the bay, by the mouth of the Carmel
River-valley, these four will remain
In the change of names. You will know it by the wild sea-fragrance of wind
Though the ocean may have climbed or retired a little;
You will know it by the valley inland that our sun and our moon were born from
Before the poles changed; and Orion in December
Evenings was strung in the throat of the valley like a lamp-lighted bridge.
Come in the morning you will see white gulls
Weaving a dance over blue water, the wane of the moon
Their dance-companion, a ghost walking
By daylight, but wider and whiter than any bird in the world.
My ghost you needn't look for; it is probably
Here, but a dark one, deep in the granite, not dancing on wind
With the mad wings and the day moon.

Arthur G. Dove. *Snow Thaw*. 1930. Oil on canvas,
18 x 24". The Phillips Collection, Washington, D.C.

From HIBERNACULUM

A. R. Ammons

the ground is practically asplatter with eavesdropping:

there are pools under the floating mush: they are not
clearly of a depth: one must know the terrain well or
fill his boots: the garage, the cold garage, and the

porch still have six inches of snow but the house across
the way whose second floor is all under a slanting roof
is snow-free: the woods, unhung completely,

have resumed an old darkness, whereas yesterday they were
still irradiated with snowholdings: the sun,
invisible before, has set into another invisibility and

the consequences are darkening here through the clouds:
oh this little time-drenched world! how it jiggles with
flickering! light as history, as relic, light two

billion years old, moves its ancient telling through
the universe and deposits right here on my grass on a
clear night dim sediment of sizable duration: that

light can be so old and far-traveled, like flint, no
prayerstone that constant, the permanent telling of
that quickness:

From LET US NOW PRAISE FAMOUS MEN
James Agee

1

. . . a house of simple people which stands empty and silent in the vast
southern country morning sunlight, and everything which on this morning in eternal
space it by chance contains, all thus left open and defenseless to a reverent and cold-
laboring spy, shines quietly forth such grandeur, such sorrowful holiness of its exacti-
tudes in existence, as no human consciousness shall ever rightly perceive, far less
impart to another: that there can be more beauty and more deep wonder in the
standings and spacings of mute furnishings on a bare floor between the squaring
bournes of walls, than in any music ever made: that this square home as it stands in
unshadowed earth between the winding years of heaven, is, not to me but of itself,
one among the serene and final, uncapturable beauties of existence: that this beauty is
made between hurt but unvanquishable nature and the plainest cruelties and needs of
human existence in this uncured time, and is inextricable among these,
and as impossible without them as a saint born in paradise.

2

There is plenty of time. We may stand here in front of it, and watch it, so
long as it may please us to; watch its wood: move and be quiet among its rooms and
meditate what the floor supports, and what is on the walls, and what is on shelves
and tables, and hangs from nails, and is in boxes and in drawers: the properties, the
relics of a human family; a human shelter: all in the special silence and
perfection which is upon a dwelling undefended of its dwellers, undisturbed; and
which is contracted between sunlight and a human shell; and in the silence and
delicateness of the shame and reverence of our searching.

Walker Evans. Interior from *Let Us Now Praise
Famous Men*. 1936. Reproduced from the
Collections of the Library of Congress,
Washington, D.C.

FAIRY TALE

Miroslav Holub
Translated from the Czech by George Theiner

He built himself a house,
      his foundations,
      his stones,
      his walls,
      his roof overhead,
      his chimney and smoke,
      his view from the window.

He made himself a garden,
      his fence,
      his thyme,
      his earthworm,
      his evening dew.

He cut out his bit of sky above.

And he wrapped the garden in the sky
and the house in the garden
and packed the lot in a handkerchief
and went off
lone as an arctic fox
through the cold
unending
rain
into the world.

Marc Chagall. *Over Vitebsk*. c. 1914.
Oil on canvas, 12⅜ x 15¾".
Philadelphia Museum of Art: The
Louis E. Stern Collection. © 1999
Artists Rights Society (ARS), New
York/ADAGP, Paris

CHIEF HOGAN SONGS

*Translated from the Navajo by Leland C. Wyman
and Brian Swann*

No. 12
I know how it is, how it goes. . . .
Now my hogan's stones are set under the doorposts
it has come into being. I know.
"Is that right?" they ask. I'm the one who knows.

William Pennington. *Navajo women in front of hogan.*
Courtesy Colorado Historical Society

Now my doorway, now my woven curtain
has come into existence. I know.
"Is that right?" they ask. I'm the one who knows.
Now long life and happiness have come into being.
I'm the one who knows.
My fire, my food, have come into being.
Now long life and happiness have come into being.
My fire, my food, have come into being.
The stirring stick, the large pot have come into being.
The big horn ladle, the big earthen bowl have come into being.
The whiskbroom, the millstone have come into being.
My bed, my woven matting have come into being.
In my hogan, in the back corners, all kinds
of precious fabrics, all kinds of jewels were brought in.
"Is that right?" they ask. I'm the one who knows.
Now long life and happiness have come into being.

No. 14
From a woman, from a woman,
it is my hogan where from the rear corners beauty radiates;
from the rear corners beauty radiates; it radiates
from a woman.
It is my hogan where from the rear center beauty radiates;
it radiates from a woman.
It is my hogan where from the fireside beauty radiates;
it radiates from a woman.
It is my hogan where from its side corners beauty radiates;
it radiates from a woman.
It is my hogan where, from the doorway, going on and on,
                                                        beauty
radiates, it radiates from a woman, its span of beauty spreads.

From SENTENCES ON THE HOUSE AND OTHER SENTENCES

John Hejduk

The house is a nocturnal thing; this is seen from the out side
       when the lights are turned on.
The house is like a black cat at night, only a silhouette.
A house roams at night when its occupants sleep.
Night dreams are accelerated in fixed rooms.
Day dreams blank out light.
The yawning of a house comes from the excessive sound of
       its inhabitants.
The house likes the weaver; it remembers its early construction.
The sister of a house is its garden.
When a house is sad its glazing clouds over and there is no
       movement of air.
The house never forgets the sound of its original occupants.
A house's ghosts stay inside; if they leave and go outside they
       disappear.
A house is only afraid of gods, fire, wind, and silence.
A house's blood is the moving people within when they still stop.
A house is seen crying when it sheds its rainwaters.
The gods are jealous of the house because the house cannot fly.
The stairs of a house are mysterious because they move up and
       down at the same time.
Snow is female, icicles male.
A house fears the wind and is afraid of trees.
A house carries its own weight, also the sorrows within.
Lightning is the house's direct connection to the heavens.

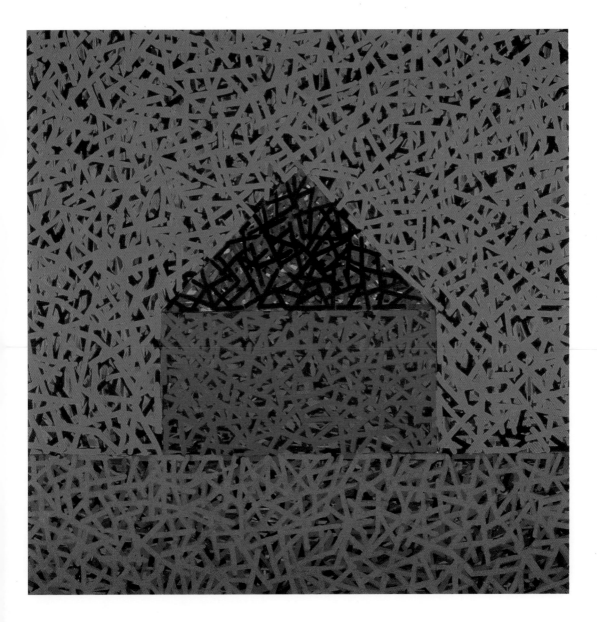

Jennifer Bartlett. *House: Open Layers*. 1997–98.
Oil on canvas, 80 x 80". Photograph courtesy the
artist. Collection Locks Gallery, Philadelphia

From THE HOUSE BEAUTIFUL

Written by William C. Gannett
Designed by Frank Lloyd Wright

Frank Lloyd Wright and Olgivanna Lloyd Wright. 1958. Courtesy
the Frank Lloyd Wright Archives, Scottsdale, Arizona

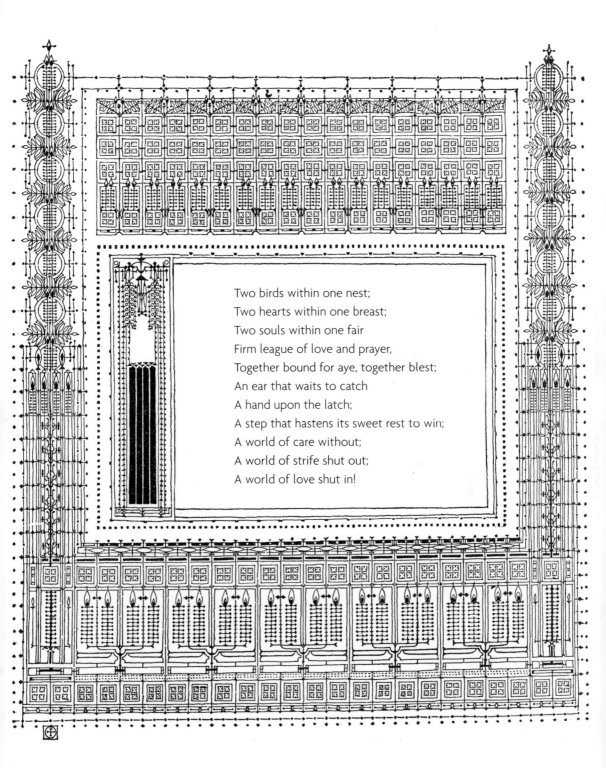

Two birds within one nest;
Two hearts within one breast;
Two souls within one fair
Firm league of love and prayer,
Together bound for aye, together blest;
An ear that waits to catch
A hand upon the latch;
A step that hastens its sweet rest to win;
A world of care without;
A world of strife shut out;
A world of love shut in!

From THE ONE DAY

Donald Hall

Smoke rises all day from two chimneys above us.
You stand by the stove looking south, through bare branches
of McIntosh, Spy, and Baldwin. You add oak logs
to the fire you built at six in the castiron stove.
At the opposite end of the same house, under another chimney,
I look toward the pond that flattens to the west
under the low sun of a January afternoon, from a notebook
busy with bushels and yields. All day in our opposite
rooms we carry wood to stoves, we pace up and down, we plan,
we set figures on paper—to converge at day's end

for kisses, bread, and talk; then we read in silence,
sitting in opposite chairs; then we turn drowsy.
Dreaming of tomorrow only, we sleep in the painted bed
while the night's frail twisting of woodsmoke assembles
overhead from the two chimneys, to mingle and disperse
as our cells will disperse and mingle when they lapse
into graveyard dirt. Meantime the day is double
in the work, love, and solitude of eyes
that gaze not at each other but at a third thing:
a child, a ciderpress, a book—work's paradise.

From north pole and south we approach each other;
Atlantic encounters Pacific, up meets down:
Where extremes meet we make our equator:—Your body
with narrow waist and carved shoulders, hips
comely, breasts outswooping; my body intent,
concentrated, and single. We enter this planisphere
without strangeness, betrayal, or risk; our bodies
after bright tumult float in shadow and repose
of watery sleep, skin's fury settling apart
and pole withdrawing to pole: A bed is the world.

Pictorial Rug. 1885–95. Germantown yarn,
74½ x 54½". Field Museum, Chicago

JERÓNIMO'S HOUSE

Elizabeth Bishop

My house, my fairy
        palace, is
of perishable
        clapboards with
three rooms in all,
        my gray wasps' nest
of chewed-up paper
        glued with spit.

My home, my love-nest,
        is endowed
with a veranda
        of wooden lace,
adorned with ferns
        planted in sponges,
and the front room
        with red and green

left-over Christmas
        decorations
looped from the corners
        to the middle
above my little
        center table
of woven wicker
        painted blue,

and four blue chairs
        and an affair
for the smallest baby
        with a tray
with ten big beads.
        Then on the walls
two palm-leaf fans
        and a calendar

and on the table
        one fried fish
spattered with burning
        scarlet sauce,
a little dish
        of hominy grits
and four pink tissue-
        paper roses.

Also I have
        hung on a hook,
an old French horn
        repainted with
aluminum paint.
        I play each year
in the parade
        for José Martí.

At night you'd think
        my house abandoned.
Come closer. You
        can see and hear
the writing-paper
        lines of light
and the voices of
        my radio

singing flamencos
        in between
the lottery numbers.
        When I move
I take these things,
        not much more, from
my shelter from
        the hurricane.

Rafael Ferrer. *El Sol Asombre*. 1989. Oil
on canvas, 60 x 72". The Butler Institute
of American Art, Youngstown, Ohio

Jan Tymorek. *Old House.* 1998

THE OLD HOUSE

William Carlos Williams

Rescued! new-white

          (from Time's
dragon: neglect-tastelessness—
the down-beat)

         But why?
why the descent into ugliness that
intervened, how
could it have come about,
             (the essence—
cluttered with weeds, broken gear
—in a shoddy neighborhood)
               something so sound?

—that there should have befallen
such decay, such decay of the senses—
the redundant and expensive,
the useless, the useless rhyme?

Stasis:
       a balance of . . .
vacuities, seeking . . . to
achieve . . . by emphasis!
the full sonorities of . . . an
evasion! !

         —lack of
"virtue," the fake castellation, the
sham tower—upon a hidden
weakness of trusses, a whole period
shot to hell out of disrelatedness
to mind, to object association:

             the years following
the Civil War—

         But four
balanced gables, in a good old style,
four symmetrical waves,
                well anchored,
turning around the roof's pivot,
simple and direct,
             how could they not
have apprehended it? They could not—
Bitter reminder.

         And then!
out of the air, out of decay, out of
desire, necessity, through
economic press—aftermath of "the bomb"—
a Perseus! rescue comes:

            —the luminous
from "sea wrack," sets it, for itself,
a house almost gone, shining again.

FABLE OF THE HOUSE

Robert Kelly

This is a house
and will be for a long time
itself because the air
has come to recognize it
and call it by name.
        "Hello, House,
the birds are getting ready
down in Bolivia to come back
and bother you again."
        With its eaves
the house is listening, "O brother,
o bother, the birds
again, and their seeds, their seeds
have trees and their trees have birds
and there we are again,
all over me and the morning
too loud for me and the men and women
running down my halls
crying for their children and their children
with birds on their knees.
O it is hard to be me, it is hard to house."

"Cheer up, brother," says the air.
"I care and care and hurry everywhere
at once, and wherever I go
are people and their things
and every thing must have its man
or woman, and every house
must have its birds. I endure the clouds
and their unseen attendants,
I endure the morning choked with light
and the evening drowned in darkness
and none of it bothers me. None of it
should bother you, after all
you are a nest of things
and what a thing is
is a kind of sleeping. Isn't that so?"

So so was it, that the house was fast asleep.

Andrew Wyeth. *Soaring*. 1950. Tempera, 48 x 87".
Shelburne Museum, Shelburne, Vermont

SOME DETAILS OF HEBRIDEAN HOUSE CONSTRUCTION

Thomas A. Clark

the walls are built with
unmortared boulders
the external faces having
an inward slope
the corners rounded

roofs are thatched with
straw, ferns or heather
and weighted with stones
hung from heather ropes

instead of overhanging
the roof is set back
on a broad wall-top
which in the course of time
becomes mantled with
grass and verdure
which may provide
occasional browsing
for a sheep or goat

back to the wind
face to the sun
is the general
orientation

the floor is of beaten earth
and the main room is reached
by way of the byre
there are no windows and
the frugal flame of the peat
gives the only illumination
smoke wanders and finds
egress by a hole in the roof

in the outer isles the floor is covered
with white sand from the machair

a few steps ascend
the wall near the door
to enable the roof
to be thatched or roped
or the family to sit
in the summer weather
and sew, chat or knit

by the peat store
near to the doorway
is placed a large stone
for the wanderer to sit on

Arthur G. Dove. *Goin' Fishin'*. 1925. Collage
on wood panel, 19½ x 24". The Phillips
Collection, Washington, D.C.

FINLAY'S HOUSE (IN ROUSAY)

Ian Hamilton Finlay

And this is Finlay's house—
A wild stone on the floor,
Lots and lots of books
And a chair where you can't sit for
—No, not the tar—
The hooks, the lost fish-hooks.

Dried fish festoon the wall
And that stone sticks the door.
Spiders spin in nooks.
The visitors tend to fall:
They trip first, then they fall—
They catch on the lost fish-hooks.

I ought to shift that stone
But it seems easier
To unscrew the door.
Am I an awful man?
I'm better housed than ducks
And like to lose fish-hooks.

HOME

Michael Hamburger

1

Red house on the hill.
Windward, the martins' mud nests
Year after year filled
With a twittering, muttering brood.
On the still side, hedged,
Apples turned in on themselves
A damp, dull summer long
Until ripe. Rare hum of bees.
The two great elms where the jackdaws roosted,
Beyond them the wild half-acre
With elm scrub rising, rambling
From old roots—
Never tamed or possessed
Though I sawed, scythed, dug
And planted saplings, walnut,
Hazel, sweet chestnut,
A posthumous grove.
And the meadow's high grass,
Flutter of day-moth over
Mallow, cranesbill, vetch:
All razed, bole and brick,
Live bough and empty nest,
Battered, wrenched, scooped
Away to be dumped, scrapped.

2

A place in the mind, one place in one or two minds
Till they move on, confused, cluttered with furniture,
    landmarks.
The house let me go in the end, sprung no more leaks or
    cracks,
The garden ceased to disown me with bindweed, ground
    elder.

What's left is whole: a sketch or two, a few photographs,
A name on old maps. And the weather. The light.

3

Seeing martins fly
Over a tiled roof, not mine,
Over concrete, tarmac,
A day-moth cling
To a nettle-flower,
Hearing children, not mine,
Call out in a laurel-hedged orchard,
I'm there again. Home.

Nell Choate Jones.
Georgia Red Clay. 1946.
Oil on canvas, 25 x 30".
Morris Museum of Art,
Augusta, Georgia

Jeffrey Becom. *Boy and Golden Wall,
Kantunil, Yucatán, Mexico.* 1994

Our land is sad and faded,
so our houses must be joyful and alive.
We like the rich yellow, burning bright as candles
in a field that is otherwise all dust and stone.

—Maya woman, Kantunil, Yucatán, Mexico

From THE DESIGN OF
THE HOUSE: IDEAL
AND HARD TIME

Wendell Berry

Winter nights the house sleeps,
a dry seedhead in the snow
falling and fallen, the white
and dark and depth of it, continuing
slow impact of silence.
      The dark
rooms hold our heads on pillows, waiting
day, through the snow falling and fallen
in the darkness between inconsecutive
dreams. The brain burrows in its earth
and sleeps,
     trusting dawn, though the sun's
light is a light without precedent, never
proved ahead of its coming, waited for
by the law that hope has made it.

Maxfield Parrish. *Dusk*. 1942. Oil on board, 13¼ x 15¼".
New Britain Museum of American Art, Charles F. Smith
Fund. New Britain, Connecticut. © Estate of Maxfield
Parrish/Licensed by ASaP and VAGA, New York

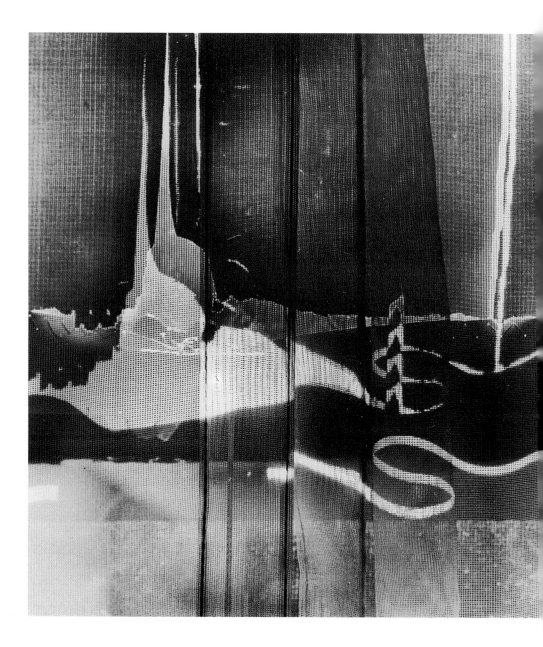

Clarence John Laughlin. *Language of Light*. 1952.
The Historic New Orleans Collection

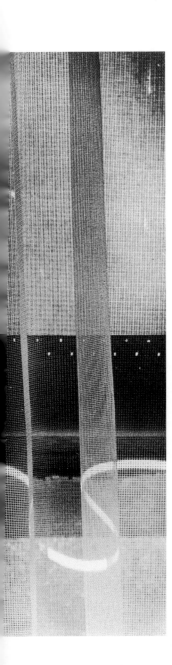

ZAGREB 1926

Christopher Middleton

The window swinging open spread a flash
Of light, splendid and warm the sun
Settled on the table cloth, the vase,
Lay on the white bed, singled out the pictures.

Hallo, light, glorious with your rays,
Hallo, linen, fragrant in your wardrobe.
Flowering cherry steeped the orchard in perfume,
Bees occupied our thoughts, honey, the pure things.

Gentleness: back and forth it ticked
And talked, like an affable old man, the pendulum.
Gentleness: the clink of cups and plates,
The smells of cream and stored apples.

And while the slanting rays explored
Crannies where the light and shadow blent,
Our funny faces, caught in the globed vase,
And a snippet of our sky gazed back at us,

In its ample curves we contemplated
Birds that flew in flocks across the town,
The roofs of all the houses turning red,
Right above the bell tower, now, the sun.

(After a Serbo-Croatian poem, "Reflections," by Ljubo Wiesner)

Edward Hopper. *Light at Two Lights.* 1927.
Watercolor on paper, 13⅞ x 19⅞". Whitney
Museum of American Art, New York.
Josephine N. Hopper Bequest

ROUND AND ROUND

Thom Gunn

The lighthouse keeper's world is round,
Belongings skipping in a ring—
All that a man may want, therein,
A wife, a wireless, bread, jam, soap,
Yet day by night his straining hope
Shoots out to live upon the sound
The spinning waves make while they break
For their own endeavour's sake—
The lighthouse keeper's world is round.

He wonders, winding up the stair
To work the lamp which lights the ships,
Why each secured possession skips
With face towards the centre turned,
From table-loads of books has learned
Shore-worlds are round as well, not square,
But there things dance with faces out-
ward turned: faces of fear and doubt?
He wonders, winding up the stair.

When it is calm, the rocks are safe
To take a little exercise
But all he does is fix his eyes
On that huge totem he has left
Where thoughts dance round what will not shift—
His secret inarticulate grief.
Waves have no sun, but are beam-caught
Running below his feet, wry salt,
When, in a calm, the rocks are safe.

MY HOUSE

From Meditations in Time of Civil War

W. B. Yeats

An ancient bridge, and a more ancient tower,
A farmhouse that is sheltered by its wall,
An acre of stony ground,
Where the symbolic rose can break in flower,
Old ragged elms, old thorns innumerable,
The sound of the rain or sound
Of every wind that blows;
The stilted water-hen
Crossing stream again
Scared by the splashing of a dozen cows;

A winding stair, a chamber arched with stone,
A grey stone fireplace with an open hearth,
A candle and written page.

Harland Walshaw. *Winding staircase in
Yeats's tower, Thoor Ballylee.* 1993

From A HYMN OF LOVE

Shaker hymn from The Gift to Be Simple
Edward D. Andrews

Love the inward, new creation,
Love the glory that it brings;
Love to lay a good foundation,
In the line of outward things.

Paul Rocheleau. *Second Floor, Shaker
Centre Family Dwelling (built 1822–1833),
South Union, Kentucky.* 1994

DREAM HOUSES I

Michael Hamburger

They have a history, dream history
Of how acquired, when occupied
And why vacated, those haunted half-ruins
Inherited only from earlier dreams,
Half-obscured by a wilderness
That once was garden or park.

The precise location, boundaries
Are dubious, as are my rights
Of freehold, leasehold, mere lodging.
For strangers have moved in,
Families, communes, beside
Those nearest to me
Now or at any time,
She who left me, she whom I left,
       whose handwriting changed, he whom frustration bent,
Each with a choice between many faces,
Youthful or aging, never estranged;
And the dead cohabit there with the living.

Yet the great hall, higher than warehouse, chapel,
Hidden behind the façade, reached
By going down—a staircase wide, bright,
Not winding—remains inaccessible,
Because unknown, to the newer tenants.
That hall, the alluring extension
Of one house alone, is the heart of them all.
Its bare walls, floor of grey stone
Untouched by furniture, offer
Pure luxury, space
Enclosed, held, not by me,
To immure a silence,

                home.

Clarence John Laughlin. *Spectral Fans.* 1946. The Historic New Orleans Collection

An emptiness?

        There they are,
Invisible, the living, the dead,
In a house inhabited once
And mislaid like a letter giving
Details, dates, movements
That could consummate love.

Every meeting is there,
Every parting, the word
Hardly whispered, more sensed
Than heard: all retained by the bare walls
Of the hidden hall in the tall house
Mine and not mine.

        Outside,
Where trees tower, meadows and heathland merge
In the foothills of high ranges,
The laughter of children hovers,
This muffled hammerbeat
Is their murdered great-grandmother, walking.

"The clothesline post is set"

Lorine Niedecker

The clothesline post is set
yet no totem-carvings distinguish the Niedecker tribe
from the rest; every seventh day they wash:
worship sun; fear rain, their neighbors' eyes;
raise their hands from ground to sky,
and hang or fall by the whiteness of their all.

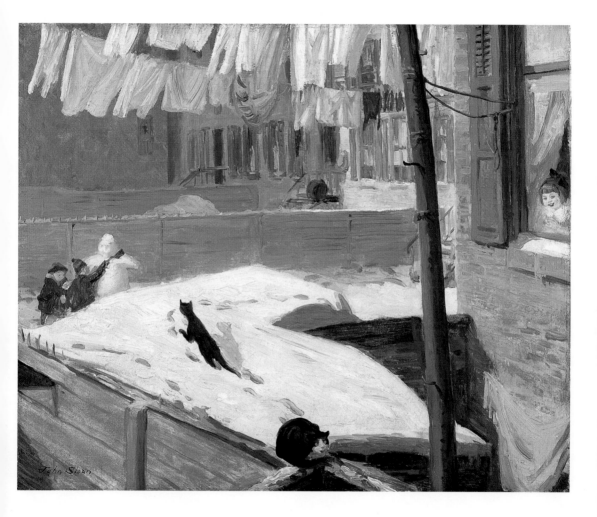

John S!oan. *Backyards, Greenwich Village.*
1914. Oil on canvas, 26 x 32". Whitney Museum
of American Art, New York

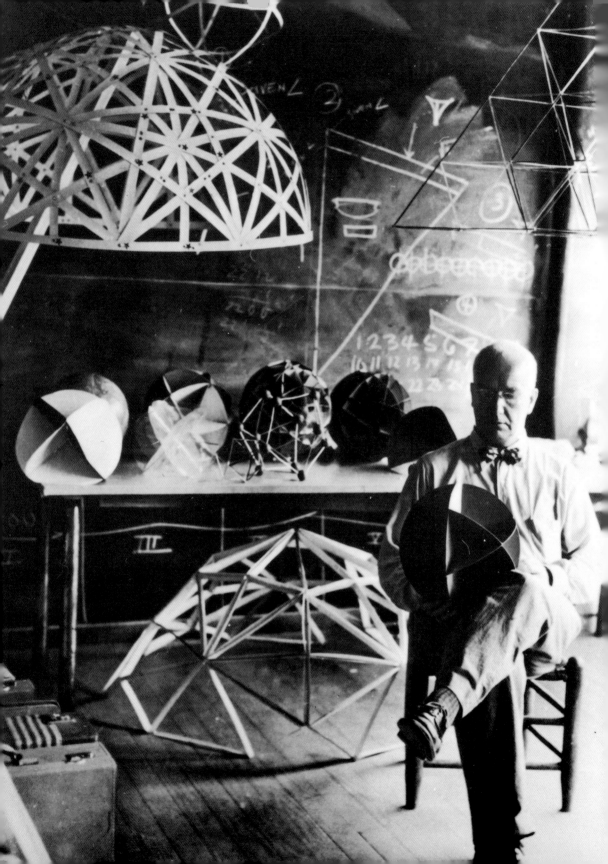

ROAM HOME TO A DOME

(Sung to the tune of "Home on the Range")
R. Buckminster Fuller

There once was a square with a romantic flare,
Pure Beaux Arts, McKim, Meade and White;
In the mood that ensued, he went factory-nude
Mies, Gropy, Corbussy, and Wright.

Roam home to a dome
Where Georgian and Gothic once stood;
Now chemical bonds alone guard our blondes.
And even the plumbing looks good.

Let architects sing of aesthetics that bring
Rich clients in hordes to their knees.
Just give me a home in a great circle dome
Where the stresses and strains are at ease.

Roam home to a dome
On the crest of a neighboring hill
Where the chores are all done, before they're begun
And eclectic nonsense is nil.

Let modern folks dream of glass boxes with steam
Out along super-burbia way;
Split-levels, split-loans, split breadwinner homes
No down money, lifetime to pay.

Roam home to a dome,
No banker would back with a dime,
No mortgage to show, no payments to go,
Where you dwell, dream, and spend only time.

Photographer unknown. *R. Buckminster Fuller at Black
Mountain College.* c. 1948. Courtesy Buckminster Fuller
Institute, Santa Barbara, California

Hilde Krassa P. *Front of La Sebastiana,*
Valparaíso, Chile. 1994. Archivo Fotografico,
Fundación Pablo Neruda

TO "LA SEBASTIANA"

Pablo Neruda
Translated from the Spanish by Alastair Reid

I built the house.

I made it first out of air.
Later I raised its flag into the air
and left it draped
from the firmament, from the stars, from
clear light and darkness.

It was a fable
of cement, iron, glass,
more valuable than wheat, like gold—
I had to go searching and selling,
and so a truck arrived.
They unloaded sacks
and more sacks.
The tower took anchor in the hard ground—
but that's not enough, said the Builder,
there's still cement, glass, iron, doors—
and I didn't sleep at night.

But it kept growing.
The windows grew,
and with a little more,
with sticking to plans and working,
and digging in with knee and shoulder,
it went on growing into existence,
to where you could look through a window,
and it seemed that with so many sacks
it might have a roof and might rise
and finally take firm hold of the flag
which still festooned the sky with its colors.

I gave myself over to the cheapest doors,
doors which had died
and had been pitched out of their houses,
doors without walls, broken,
piled up on scrap heaps,
doors with no memory by now,
no trace of a key,
and I said, "Come
to me, abandoned doors.
I'll give you a house and a wall
and a fist to knock on you.
You will swing again as the soul opens,
you will guard the sleep of Matilde
with your wings that worked so much."

Then, too, came the paint,
licking away at the walls;
it dressed them in sky blue and pink
so that they might begin to dance.
So the tower dances,
the doors and staircases sing,
the house rises till it touches its crown,
but money is short—
nails are short,
door knockers, locks, marble.
Nevertheless, the house
keeps on rising
and something happens, a beat
starts up in its arteries.
Perhaps it is a saw, seething

like a fish in the water of dreams,
or a hammer which taps
like a tricky condor carpenter
at the pine planks we will be walking on.

Something goes and living continues.

The house grows and speaks,
stands on its own feet,
has clothes wrapped round its skeleton,
and as from seaward the spring,
swimming like a water nymph,
kisses the sand of Valparaíso,

now we can stop thinking. This is the house.

Now all that's missing will be blue.

All it needs now is to bloom.

And that is work for the spring.

From CHOMEI AT TOYAMA

Basil Bunting

The dew evaporates from my sixty years,
I have built my last house, or hovel,
a hunter's bivouac, an old
silkworm's cocoon:
ten feet by ten, seven high: and I,
reckoning it a lodging not a dwelling,
omitted the usual foundation ceremony.

I have filled the frames with clay,
set hinges at the corners;
easy to take it down and carry it away
when I get bored with this place.
Two barrowloads of junk
and the cost of a man to shove the barrow,
no trouble at all.

Katsushika Hokusai (Japanese, 1760–1849). *Waterfall Series: The Ono Waterfall on the Kisokaido Road*. The Art Institute of Chicago. Gift of Mr. Chester Wright

Since I have trodden Hino mountain
noon has beaten through the awning
over my bamboo balcony, evening
shone on Amida.
I have shelved my books above the window,
lute and mandolin near at hand,
piled bracken and a little straw for bedding,
a smooth desk where the light falls, stove for bramblewood.
I have gathered stones, fitted
stones for a cistern, laid bamboo
pipes. No woodstack,
wood enough in the thicket.

Toyama, snug in the creepers!
Toyama, deep in the dense gully, open
westward whence the dead ride out of Eden
squatting on blue clouds of wistaria.
(Its scent drifts west to Amida.)

Summer? Cuckoo's *Follow, follow*—to
harvest Purgatory hill!
Fall? The nightgrasshopper will
shrill *Fickle life*!
Snow will thicken on the doorstep,
melt like a drift of sins.
No friend to break silence,
no one will be shocked if I neglect the rite.
There's a Lent of commandments kept
where there's no way to break them.

A ripple of white water after a boat,
shining water after the boats Mansami saw
rowing at daybreak
at Okinoya.
Between the maple leaf and the caneflower
murmurs the afternoon—Po Lo-tien
saying goodbye on the verge of Jinyo river.
(I am playing scales on my mandolin.)
Be limber, my fingers, I am going to play *Autumn Wind*
to the pines, I am going to play *Hastening Brook*
to the water. I am no player
but there's nobody listening,
I do it for my own amusement.

Sixteen and sixty, I and the gamekeeper's boy,
one zest and equal, chewing tsubana buds,
one zest and equal, persimmon, pricklypear,
ears of sweetcorn pilfered from Valley Farm.

The view from the summit: sky bent over Kyoto,
picnic villages, Fushimi and Toba:
a very economical way of enjoying yourself.
Thought runs along the crest, climbs Sumiyama;
beyond Kasatori it visits the great church,
goes on pilgrimage to Ishiyama (no need to foot it!)
or the graves of poets, of Semimaru who said:

> *Somehow or other*
> *we scuttle through a lifetime.*
> *Somehow or other*
> *neither palace nor straw-hut*
> *is quite satisfactory.*

René Magritte. *Personal Values*. 1952.
Oil on canvas, 31½ x 39⅜". © 1999
C. Herscovici, Brussels/Artists Rights
Society (ARS), New York

THE SKYLIGHT

From GLANMORE REVISITED
Seamus Heaney

You were the one for skylights. I opposed
Cutting into the seasoned tongue-and-groove
Of pitch pine. I liked it low and closed,
Its claustrophobic, nest-up-in-the-roof
Effect. I liked the snuff-dry feeling,
The perfect, trunk-lid fit of the old ceiling.
Under there, it was all hutch and hatch.
The blue slates kept the heat like midnight thatch.

But when the slates came off, extravagant
Sky entered and held surprise wide open.
For days I felt like an inhabitant
Of that house where the man sick of the palsy
Was lowered through the roof, had his sins forgiven,
Was healed, took up his bed and walked away.

CANTAR

Miguel Hernandez
Translated from the Spanish by Edwin Honig

The house is a dovecote,
the bed a patch of jasmine.
The door wide open with
the whole wide world beyond.

The child, your motherly heart
grown larger and larger.
There inside the room
all that's ever bloomed.

The child turns you into a garden
and you, wife, turn him into
a room full of jasmine,
a dovecote of roses.

Around your skin I tighten
and loosen my own.
A high noon of honey
you exude: a high noon.

Who entered this house
and kept it fertile?
So that I may recall—
someone I am and he's died.

Roundest light comes through
the whitest almond trees.
Life the light sinks down
with dead men and ravines.

The future is full of promise
like those horizons of
porphyry, pure marble,
where the mountains breathe.

The burning house is aflame
with kisses and lover's shadow.
Living could not be deeper
nor more compelling.

In silent overflow, milk
lights up your bones,
and the house with child and kisses
is flooded with it.

You with your swollen womb,
your child and dovecote.
Wife, over upon your husband
the sea's footsteps resound.

Archie Lieberman. *Jim, Bill and Dorothy Hammer.* 1962

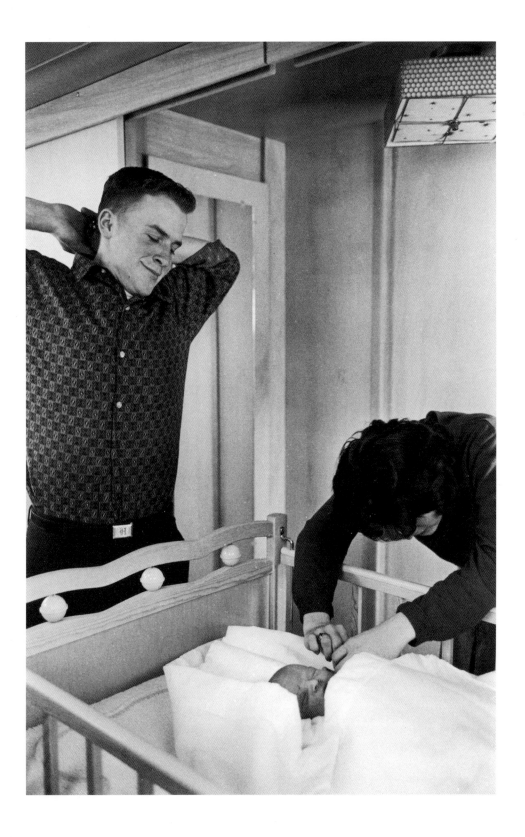

1921/24 Zimmer perspective mit Einwohner.

"House of umbrage, house of fear"

Derek Walcott

House of umbrage, house of fear,
house of multiplying air

House of memories that grow
like shadows out of Allan Poe

House where marriages go bust,
house of telephone and lust

House of caves, behind whose door
a wave is crouching with its roar

House of toothbrush, house of sin,
of branches scratching "Let me in!"

House whose rooms echo with rain,
of wrinkled clouds with Onan's stain

House that creaks, age fifty-seven,
wooden earth and plaster heaven

House of channelled CableVision
whose dragoned carpets sneer derision

Unlucky house that I uncurse
by rites of genuflecting verse

House I unhouse, house that can harden
as cold as stones in the lost garden

House where I look down the scorched street
but feel its ice ascend my feet

I do not live in you, I bear
my house inside me, everywhere

until your winters grow more kind
by the dancing firelight of mind

where knobs of brass do not exist,
whose doors dissolve with tenderness

House that lets in, at last, those fears
that are its guests, to sit on chairs

feasts on their human faces, and
takes pity simply by the hand

shows her her room, and feels the hum
of wood and brick becoming home.

Paul Klee. *Perspective of a Room with
Inhabitants.* 1921. Oil and watercolor,
19⅕ x 12 ⅗". Kuntsmuseum, Bern

UPLAND HOUSE

W. S. Merwin

The door was not even locked and all through the day
      light came in between the boards as it had always done
through each of the lives there the one life of sunlight slipping
      so slowly that it would have appeared to be
not moving if anyone had been there to notice
      but they were all gone by then while it went on tracing the way
by heart over the cupped floorboards the foot of the dark bed
      in the corner the end of the table covered
with its crocheted cloth once white and the dishes yet on it
      candlestick bottles stain under one bulge in the black
ceiling the ranges of cobwebs roots of brambles
      fingering the fireplace the line continued across them
in silence not taking anything with it as
      it travelled through its own transparent element
I watched it move and everything I remembered
      had happened in a country with a different language
and when I remembered that house I would not be the same

Robert Rauschenberg. *Quiet House, Black Mountain.* c. 1949.
© Robert Rauschenberg / Licensed by VAGA, New York

THE ACCUMULATION

James Laughlin

I'm looking down on them, my
children and my grandchildren,
as they struggle to get rid
of all the mess I've left
accumulated in the house. "My
god," they sigh, "couldn't
he have gotten rid of some
of these books and magazines
while he was still around to
know who would want them?"
Did he ever throw away a book
that was sent to him by some
struggling writer? The people
from the Salvation Army came
to look at them. They threw up
their hands in astonishment.
They estimated there were
fifteen hundred linear feet
of shelving full of books.
It would take ten truckloads
to cart them away and then
there would be the problem
of disposing of them. They
said the EPA had strict laws
for disposing of paper without
smoking up the atmosphere.
Where I was I couldn't give
any advice. And if I could
communicate what would I say?
I would just have to plead
I suffered from bibliomania.
A long life of bibliomania
and now no way to make
up for it.

From THE OLD POET MOVES TO A NEW APARTMENT 14 TIMES

Louis Zukofsky

When the walls
are dismantled
realize
the horror
of dust

but also
where a curtain
kept the dust from
the walls,
a white

that with most
things   packed   shows   how
little one needs
waiting for the movers

to come.

From SNOW-BOUND

John Greenleaf Whittier

Shut in from all the world without,
We sat the clean-winged hearth about,
Content to let the north-wind roar
In baffled rage at pane and door,
While the red logs before us beat
The frost-line back with tropic heat;
And ever, when a louder blast
Shook beam and rafter as it passed,
The merrier up its roaring draught
The great throat of the chimney laughed;
The house-dog on his paws outspread
Laid to the fire his drowsy head,
The cat's dark silhouette on the wall
A couchant tiger's seemed to fall;
And, for the winter fireside meet,
Between the andirons' straddling feet,
The mug of cider simmered slow,
The apples sputtered in a row,
And, close at hand, the basket stood
With nuts from brown October's wood.

What matter how the night behaved?
What matter how the north-wind raved?
Blow high, blow low, not all its snow
Could quench our hearth-fire's ruddy glow.

Paul Rocheleau. *Ulster Irish Farm, Museum of
American Frontier Culture, Staunton, Virginia.* 1994

Jan Tymorek. *Bedroom at Loeb Farm.* 1988

MY ROOM

Patrick Kavanagh

10 by 12
And a low roof
If I stand by the side wall
My head feels the reproof.

Five holy pictures
Hang on the walls:
The Virgin and Child
St Anthony of Padua
Leo the XIII
St Patrick and the Little Flower.

My bed in the centre
So many things to me—
A dining table
A writing desk
And a slumber palace.

My room in a dusty attic
But its little window
Lets in the stars.

From THE ALHAMBRA INSCRIPTION

Ibn Zamrak
Translated by Christopher Middleton and
Leticia Garza-Falcón from Spanish versions
of the original Arabic

The palace portico, so beautiful
It bids to rival heaven's very vault;
Clothed in a woven raiment fine as this
You can forget the busy looms of Yemen.
See what arches mount upon its roof
And spring from columns burnished by the light
Like the celestial spheres that turn and turn
Above the luminous column of the dawn.
Altogether the columns are so beautiful
That every tongue is telling their renown;
Black the shadow-darkened cornice cuts
Across the fair light thrown by snowy marble;
Such opalescent shimmers swarm about,
You'd say, for all their size, they are of pearl.
Never have we seen a palace rise so high,
With such a clarity, such expanse of outline;
Never did a garden brim like this with flowers,
Fruits more sweet to taste or more perfumed.
It pays the fee required of beauty's critic
Twice and in two varieties of coin:
For if, at dawn, an early breeze will toss
Into his hands drachmas of light galore,
Later, in the thick of tree and shrub,
With coins of gold the sun will lavish him.
What sired these kindred things? A victory:
Still none can match the lineage of the king.

Adam Lubroth. *Court of the Lions*. 14th c.,
Nasrid Dynasty. Alhambra, Granada, Spain

From THE COTTER'S SATURDAY NIGHT

(Inscribed to R. Aiken, Esq.)
Robert Burns

2

November chill blaws loud wi' angry sugh;
      The short'ning winter-day is near a close;
The miry beasts retreating frae the pleugh;
      The black'ning trains o' craws to their repose:
      The toil-worn Cotter frae his labor goes,
This night his weekly moil is at an end,
      Collects his spades, his mattocks, and his hoes,
Hoping the morn in ease and rest to spend,
And weary, o'er the moor, his course does
        hameward bend.

3

At length his lonely Cot appears in view,
      Beneath the shelter of an aged tree;
The' expectant wee-things, toddlan, stacher
        through
      To meet their Dad, wi' flichterin noise and
        glee.
      His wee bit ingle, blinkan bonilie,
His clean hearth-stane, his thrifty Wifie's smile,
      The lisping infant, prattling on his knee,
Does a' his weary kiaugh and care beguile,
And makes him quite forget his labor and his
        toil.

Harland Walshaw. *Burns's Cottage, Alloway.* 1993

NEW STANZAS FOR
AMAZING GRACE

Allen Ginsberg

I dreamed I dwelled in a homeless place
Where I was lost alone
Folk looked right through me into space
And passed with eyes of stone.

O homeless hand on many a street
Accept this change from me
A friendly smile or word is sweet
As fearless charity

Woe workingman who hears the cry
And cannot spare a dime
Nor look into a homeless eye
Afraid to give the time

So rich or poor no gold to talk
A smile on your face
The homeless ones where you may walk
Receive amazing grace

I dreamed I dwelled in a homeless place
Where I was lost alone
Folk looked right through me into space
And passed with eyes of stone

Eric Drooker. *The Crowd.* 1996

HOUSECOOLING

William Matthews

Those ashes shimmering dully in the fireplace,
like tarnished fish scales? I swept them out.
Those tiny tumbleweeds of dust that stalled
against a penny or a paperclip under the bed?
I lay along the grain of the floorboards
and stared each pill into the vacuum's mouth.
I loved that house and I was moving out.

What do you want to do when you grow up?
they asked, and I never said, *I want to haunt
a house.* But I grew pale. The way the cops "lift"
fingerprints, that's how I touched the house.
The way one of my sons would stand in front
of me and say, *I'm outta here,* and he would mean
it, his crisp, heart-creasing husk delivering

a kind of telegram from wherever the rest of him
had gone — that's how I laved and scoured
and patrolled the house, and how I made my small
withdrawals and made my wan way outta there.
And then I was gone. I took what I could.
Each smudge I left, each slur, each whorl, I left
for love, but love of what I cannot say.

Ralph Eugene Meatyard. *Untitled.* 1966.
Courtesy Howard Greenberg Gallery, New York

Horace Pippin. *Cabin in the Cotton.*
Mid-1930s. Oil on panel, 18⅛ x 33⅛". The
Art Institute of Chicago. In memoriam:
Frances W. Pick from her children Thomas
F. Pick and Mary P. Hines

NO TOOL OR ROPE OR PAIL

Bob Arnold

It hardly mattered what time of year
We passed by their farmhouse,
They never waved,
This old farm couple
Usually bent over in the vegetable garden
Or walking the muddy dooryard
Between house and red-weathered barn.
They would look up, see who was passing,
Then look back down, ignorant to the event.
We would always wave nonetheless,
Before you dropped me off at work
Further up on the hill,
Toolbox rattling in the backseat,
And then again on the way home
Later in the day, the pale sunlight
High up in their pasture,
Our arms out the window,
Cooling ourselves.
And it was that one midsummer evening
We drove past and caught them sitting
Together on the front porch
At ease, chores done,
The tangle of cats and kittens
Cleaning themselves of fresh spilled milk
On the barn door ramp;
We drove by and they looked up—
The first time I've ever seen their
Hands free of any work,
No tool or rope or pail—
And they waved.

THE HOMEPLACE

Lenard D. Moore

When I walk the path this morning
there is only a slight light
in the thinned woods.
I come upon a creek
near a tin-roofed house;
and there's no one anywhere
to witness my presence.

Meanwhile the wind
rises through the branches—
but soon reaches groundfall.
A faint smell of honeysuckle
sustains itself on the air
while quail rove the slope-weeds.
My eyes will not let go.

Now I think of my great-grandfather
who one time walked these woods through daylight.
This is the country he knew since boyhood.
And I am grateful for this homeplace—
here, I, too, wish to grow old
and stand without words
in this part of the world
so lively and pure.

I can hear a dog barking
somewhere in the far distance—
here where the voices of former life
do not speak, their spirits huddling
into themselves, a brotherhood of saints.
We are this fresh green world
which cradles everything into itself.

Archie Lieberman. *Misty Field.* 1961

Rita Lanham, age 10. *Imagining Grace's House.*
1998. Colored pencil on paper

GRACE'S HOUSE

Thomas Merton

On the summit: it stands on a fair summit
Prepared by winds: and solid smoke
Rolls from the chimney like a snow cloud.
Grace's house is secure.

No blade of grass is not counted,
No blade of grass forgotten on this hill.
Twelve flowers make a token garden.
There is no path to the summit—
No path drawn
To Grace's house.

All the curtains are arranged
Not for hiding but for seeing out.
In one window someone looks out and winks.
Two gnarled short
Fortified trees have knotholes
From which animals look out.
From behind a corner of Grace's house
Another creature peeks out.

Important: hidden in the foreground
Most carefully drawn
The dog smiles, his foreleg curled, his eye like an aster.
Nose and collar are made with great attention:
This dog is loved by Grace!

And there: the world!
Mailbox number 5
Is full of Valentines for Grace.
There is a name on the box, name of a family
Not yet ready to be written in language.

A spangled arrow there
Points from our Coney Island
To her green sun-hill.

Between our world and hers
Runs a sweet river:
(No, it is not the road,
It is the uncrossed crystal
Water between our ignorance and her truth.)

O paradise, O child's world!
Where all the grass lives
And all the animals are aware!
The huge sun, bigger than the house
Stands and streams with life in the east
While in the west a thunder cloud
Moves away forever.

No blade of grass is not blessed
On this archetypal hill,
This womb of mysteries.

I must not omit to mention a rabbit
And two birds, bathing in the stream
Which is no road, because

Alas, there is no road to Grace's house!

From THE BUNKER IN THE PARSLEY FIELDS

Gary Gildner
(written in Czechoslovakia, 1992)

I am in the Parsley Fields, six floors up
watching this boy straight down bang his trike
over and over: he rolls back, waits a moment gathering
steam, then head lowered, a little bull, pedals hard
smack into the bunker again. It doesn't budge, of course, it
sits there more solid than Papa, the size
of a soccer field, roofless, as high above ground
as the boy is tall, walls so thick he can
lie across them anywhere and not hang over, deep
as two or three placid elephants standing one
on top the other, making no sound, no raised trumpet calls,
no crap, what would the boy think of a trick like that?
       This bunker, these
stacked-up flats where thousands cook and stew
and see inside the box another queen take home a perfect ermine
fur, an airline ticket, stuff to cream, color, butter, and dust
herself all over, stretch for miles along the Danube—
into a repetition that shimmers at the ends
as heat shimmers on the summer highway just ahead
and makes your eyes water if you look too long. And it's
called the Parsley Fields, this place, not because in the Greek root
parsley means rock and stone, but because
once upon a time some people can still remember
that delicate herb declared itself abundantly on these banks,

Elizabeth Sloan. *Moon over Sečov.*
1992. Oil pastel, 14 x 17"

where in the early hours our tenor neighbor upstairs
will wake us calling softly for Carmen
and finish off by screaming nothing not even wretched
Don José would understand, as if an old poem
he had written on coarse paper, or a rope,
got stuck in his throat,
where the moon spreads out
at the bottom of a hard, wet notion
that now official change has come
no one knows what to do with except this boy
who rams and rams it wearing
three little ruts in the mud.

MYSTERIES OF SMALL HOUSES

Alice Notley

Poverty much maligned but beautiful
has resulted in smaller houses replete with mysteries
How can something so finite
so petite and shallow have
the infinite center I sense there? There

in the alley house for example
I enter it again, utterly still in the morning and with
shadows around its door mouth and throughout
frontroom bedroom diningroom kitchen room of washtubs and
porch made my room, all
small, small and worn linoleum blue pattern pink
flowers, but now it's all shadows
'cause inside its center I'm, or is it we're
It's I'm that I won't ever know
completely unless I do when I die

William Gedney. *Untitled (Girls in the Kitchen, Eastern Kentucky).* 1964.
William Gedney Collection, Rare Book, Manuscript, and Special
Collections Library, Duke University, Durham, North Carolina

How

    do

we manage to base ourselves on dark ignorance so
house of pressed-down pushed-in
origin, is such poverty; or
apartments where people die, again the strange dense
center of the four tiny rooms on St. Mark's Place may be that
Ted died there and so left a mystery vortex inside that fragile
apartment on stilts—Doug, do you think so?

                                      you

lived there. This apartment where we are now isn't
so poor, though it's small
The house must be small and fragile
My grandparents' house too had four small rooms
and no bath or shower and whenever you sat on the
toilet a mynah bird across the lot cried out
Their house had a darkness where they slept

I know I'm not talking about poverty exactly but not
having, why have it's such
an illusion, and the body-self such a shadowy fragile house—

Go in and find that room that secret
is it under it   or inside, it's inside a shadow
if I could just slip into it—and if I do I'm still whole but
mum in old Needles
the motel's too big the churches are too and the mute
low-lying schools
there's the desert beyond them that I try to keep housed from
no thin flesh there no coursing fluid no thought

From URBANAL

Christopher Logue

      The slippery whinnock,* clear across the way,
Has had my tree cut down.
He rang a man who rang a man who knew
A big-boned, broad-backed chap; the type of clay
That stood in red in line at Waterloo.
It took eight hours to knock King Boney down,
And more than 30 years to rear my tree;
But only fifteeen dental seconds flat
For that, fat, jelly-baby-faced,
Pornocrat to have it stapped.
      Now I can see his house.
A snot-brown, lie-priced, isometric blob
Smack in the middle of my laureate eye.
A yawning house, a stealthily maintained,
And as (God stop his heart) he skives abroad
A semi-empty house. His swap. Who had my tree's
Shoulders that made the evening summer breeze
Hiss like a milky night-tide up the sand
Cut down to save his garage.
      Its roots were getting at his garage.
His garage was endangered. Furthermore,
Come autumn, when the bronzed wing in, his car
Might get its chrome trim splashed with flock.
      What can I do?
Twice 20,000** square in legal blue
Behind the leaves that bear his signature
And all my leaves away.

*Smallest pig in a litter.

**Number of British police in 1975.

Jan Tymorek. *Apple Tree at Loeb Farm.* 1988

True, there are quits.
Through the enormous windows of his house
Soon after dusk when all was still and glad,
Five weeks ago I tingled as I watched
A no less sturdy, somewhat different lad,
Slither the cutlery into his bag
And fade. And Sunday last
(Meantime his nanny milked my breakfast tea)
His 'Me! Me' squeakers did their peevish best
To baste each other's shop-washed goldilux
With Hong-toy-Kong posh hand-assembled trucks.
        Such treats, however, will not quash his crime:
Indubitably I would have
Him and his pimply mouthpiece taken out
Put up against that garage wall, and shot,
If all those lads in red and blue were mine.

        And yet I did not know my tree too well.
I did not know its name; its proper age;
Whether its leaflike slips of polished silk
Were toothed or bayed, or if its full, fresh snood,
Brotherly hugged, flushed leek down green imperial;
Or did that gust strike dark down adder green?—
How much it gained each year; how high it stood;
Or standing might have fetched that fleshy hood,
Except he had it lamed, laid, lopped, and logged:
'Just for the wood'.

Lonny Schiff. *Moonbase*. 1998.
Monoprint and collage, 22 x 20".
Courtesy Kelly Barrette Fine Arts

A HOME IN SPACE

Edwin Morgan

Laid-back in orbit, they found their minds.
They found their minds were very clean and clear.
Clear crystals in swarms outside were their fireflies and larks.
Larks they were in lift-off, swallows in soaring.
Soaring metal is flight and nest together.
Together they must hatch.
Hatches let the welders out.
Out went the whitesuit riggers with frames as light as air.
Air was millions under lock and key.
Key-ins had computers wild on Saturday nights.
Nights, days, months, years they lived in space.
Space shone black in their eyes.
Eyes, hands, food-tubes, screens, lenses, keys were one.

One night—or day—or month—or year—they all—
all gathered at the panel and agreed—
agreed to cut communication with—
with the earth base—and it must be said they were—
were cool and clear as they dismantled the station and—
and gave their capsule such power that—
that they launched themselves outwards—
outwards in an impeccable trajectory, that band—
that band of tranquil defiers, not to plant any—
any home with roots but to keep a—
a voyaging generation voyaging, and as far—
as far as there would ever be a home in space—
space that needs time and time that needs life.

INDEX OF POETS

INDEX OF ARTISTS

POETRY CREDITS

Grateful acknowledgment is made for permission to reproduce the poems and excerpts from texts by the following writers. All possible care has been taken to trace ownership of every selection included and to make full acknowledgment. If any errors or omissions have occurred, they will be corrected in subsequent editions, provided that notification is sent to the publisher.

James Agee, *Let Us Now Praise Famous Men.* Copyright © 1939, 1940 by James Agee. Copyright © 1941 by James Agee and Walker Evans. Copyright © renewed 1969 by Mila Fritsch Agee and Walker Evans. Reprinted by permission of Houghton Mifflin Co. All rights reserved

A. R. Ammons, "Hibernaculum," from *Collected Poems 1951–1971* by A. R. Ammons. Copyright © 1972 by A. R. Ammons. Reprinted by permission of W. W. Norton & Company, Inc.

Bob Arnold, "No Tool or Rope or Pail" and "Prize" reprinted by permission of Bob Arnold from *Where Rivers Meet* (Mad River Press, 1990)

Jeffrey Becom and Sally Jean Aberg, Maya woman quote from *Maya Color: The Painted Villages of Mesoamerica.* Copyright © 1997 Abbeville Press, New York. Reprinted by permission of the authors

Wendell Berry, "The Design of the House: Ideal and Hard Time" from *Selected Poems of Wendell Berry.* Copyright © 1998 Wendell Berry. Reprinted by permission of Counterpoint Press

Elizabeth Bishop, "Jerónimo's House" from *The Complete Poems 1927–1979* by Elizabeth Bishop. Copyright © 1979, 1983 by Alice Helen Methfessel. Reprinted by permission of Farrar, Straus & Giroux, Inc.

William Bronk, "My House New-painted." Copyright © William Bronk. Reprinted by permission of William Bronk

Basil Bunting, "Chomei at Toyama" from *The Complete Poems of Basil Bunting* (1994). Copyright © 1994 The Estate

of Basil Bunting. Reprinted by permission of Oxford University Press

Thomas A. Clark, "Some Details of Hebridean House Construction" from *Tormentil and Bleached Bones.* Copyright © 1993 Thomas A. Clark. Reprinted by permission of Edinburgh University Press

Robert Creeley, "This House" from *Echoes.* Copyright © 1994 by Robert Creeley. Reprinted by permission of New Directions Publishing Corp.

Emily Dickinson, "I years had been from home." Reprinted by permission of the publishers and the Trustees of Amherst College from *The Poems of Emily Dickinson*, Thomas H. Johnson, ed., Cambridge, Mass.: The Belknap Press of Harvard University Press, Copyright © 1951, 1955, 1979, 1983 by the President and Fellows of Harvard College

Ian Hamilton Finlay, "Finlay's House (at Rousay)" from *The Dancers Inherit the Party.* Copyright © 1996 by Ian Hamilton Finlay. Reprinted by permission of Edinburgh University Press

R. Buckminster Fuller, "Roam Home to a Dome." Copyright © The Estate of R. Buckminster Fuller. Reprinted by permission of The Estate of R. Buckminster Fuller

Forrest Gander, "The Ark Upon His Shoulders" from *Science & Steepleflower.* Copyright © 1997 by Forrest Gander. Reprinted by permission of New Directions Publishing Corp.

Willian C. Gannett and Frank Lloyd Wright, quote from *The House Beautiful.* Courtesy The Frank Lloyd Wright Archives, Scottsdale, Arizona

Gary Gildner, "The Bunker in the Parsley Fields" from *The Bunker in the Parsley Fields* (University of Iowa Press, 1997). Copyright © 1997 by Gary Gildner. Reprinted by permission of the author

Allen Ginsberg, "New Stanzas for *Amazing Grace*" from *Selected Poems 1947–1995* by Allen Ginsberg. Copyright

PHOTOGRAPH CREDITS

ILLUSTRATION COPYRIGHTS